CREDIT–LIT SERIES

The Credit-Lit Monthly Planner
for Getting and Maintaining Good Credit

Dionne Perry
Board Certified Credit Consultant

Instill Publishing
Atlanta, GA

Instill Publishing
Atlanta, GA
www.InstillPublishingcom
www.Credit-Lit.com

ISBN 978-1-7359470-2-0 Softcover Edition

ISBN 978-1-7359470-3-7 Spiral Edition

Cover and interior design: Anita Jones anotherjones.com

Printed in the United States of America

Welcome to The Credit-Lit Planner

A credit score impacts every financial decision you make. Many consumers haven't understood how and why credit scores affect their lives...until now!

This Credit-Lit Planner is designed for adults of any age and is a trusted, valuable resource to help you achieve great credit! From tracking and monitoring your credit score to recording your monthly income and supervising your savings and debts – our Planner teaches you the critical elements you need to know to grow and maintain excellent credit. It also includes a glossary of terms to define and clarify as you read through the early sections.

This Planner gives you the opportunity to develop healthy monthly habits, monetary strategies, and action plans over 12 months. Not only is the Credit-Lit Planner a great resource for you to learn, but we also provide Money Affirmations and Quotes to make sure you stay motivated every step of the way.

The Credit-Lit Planner is undated, allowing you to achieve the credit score of your dreams starting at any point in time. Thanks to its convenient size, it fits in any bag, allowing you to track your finances anywhere, anytime.

This Planner is designed for easy and effective budget planning and is accessible to everyone. The practical features combined with the inspirational quotes keep you focused on the goal of achieving excellent credit.

Dionne Perry, a board-certified Credit Consultant, and a national award winning author, delivers the goods on credit, giving adults, youth and teens exactly what they need to make it in this economy.

With a Master's degree in Human Resources, a Bachelor's degree in Education, Training, and Development, plus experience as a licensed mortgage broker, Perry is uniquely qualified to educate adults and young people on the importance of maintaining a good credit score. Over the past twenty-five years, she's dedicated time and effort to doing exactly that!

Perry writes and speaks on the subject of credit and all its forms. As a Credit-Litologist, she can be heard on podcasts and at virtual and in-person events at businesses, organizations, schools, and libraries.

www.InstillPublishing.com
www.Credit-Lit.com

PART ONE

Understanding Your Credit Score and Credit Report and How It Impacts Your Life!

What Is Credit?

Credit means being able to borrow money to purchase goods and services when you may not have the cash to cover the cost at that moment.

Credit is considered a loan with the understanding that the monetary balance will be paid back in accordance with the loan agreement set up by the lender (i.e., person, bank, or company) where you obtained the line of credit. The lender can also be referred to as the creditor. A line of credit is the amount of money a financial institution, like a bank or company, has agreed to lend you.

Whether or not you are granted credit is based upon your past history with borrowing and repaying creditors. Are you trustworthy? If you are issued a line of credit, will you pay the loan back on time?

CREDIT DEFINED

How To Get Credit?

To apply for a line of credit you must be at least 18 years old and receive enough steady income (i.e., monthly) from an employer or your business.

There are different ways you can apply for credit and different reasons you need credit. Here is a list of a few reasons you might need credit as a young adult or adult.

- Auto Loans
- Credit Cards
- Mortgage Loans
- Student Loans

When borrowing money, you don't just pay the original loan amount back, you also pay the interest. For example, if you apply for a line of credit to purchase a new laptop, you're responsible for paying the initial purchase (cost of the laptop) and the interest on the money you borrowed to purchase the laptop.

Credit Guidelines Include Making a Plan

Different creditors may have different guidelines for lending credit based on their company's specific needs. However, one thing all creditors have in common is that they want:

1. The borrower to pay the agreed upon payments on time.
2. If the borrower doesn't pay the agreed upon payments on time, the lender will report a late payment on the borrower's credit report.

At the time of purchase, you do not have to pay the balance (the whole amount) of whatever **goods (i.e., laptop, cell phone, automobile, home)** or services you acquire, but you ARE responsible for repaying the loan amount over time.

Before you can purchase an item or service through taking out a line of credit, you need to have an agreement that tells you how and when you must pay back the loan. This is known as a payment plan/agreement. It tells you, very specifically, how you are to pay and by what date.

Different Types of Credit

Revolving Credit:
Revolving credit is a type of <u>credit</u> that does not have a fixed number of payments. For example, credit card accounts are considered revolving credit. You can continue to make purchases while you pay on the balances.

Installment Credit:
Installment credit is a type of agreement or contract that involves a loan to be repaid over a certain amount of time with a set number of scheduled payments. For example, a car loan is considered installment credit. It's just for one purchase at a time.

Open Credit:
Open credit is a pre-approved loan between a lender and a borrower. Open credit usually allows a borrower to make repeated withdrawals up to a certain limit. A personal loan is an example of open credit.

Credit Score and How It's Calculated

A credit score is a number that lenders use to help them decide how likely it is that they will be repaid in a timely manner.

In order to calculate your credit score, creditors often use the Fair, Isaac, and Company (FICO) score. This score is based upon the information gathered from each of the big three agencies: Equifax, Transunion and Experian.

Once the information is retrieved, the formula percentage of each component is broken down as follows:
- 35% Payment History
- 30% Current loan and Credit Card debt
- 15% Length of Credit History
- 10% Types of Credit
- 10% New Credit

FICO scores are between 300-850. In order to be considered to have good credit using your FICO score, you would need at least a 670. A score of 700 or above is generally considered very good.

For Experian, a score of 800 or above is considered exceptional for consumers and businesses, based on a scale ranging from 300-850. A score of 700 or above is considered good.

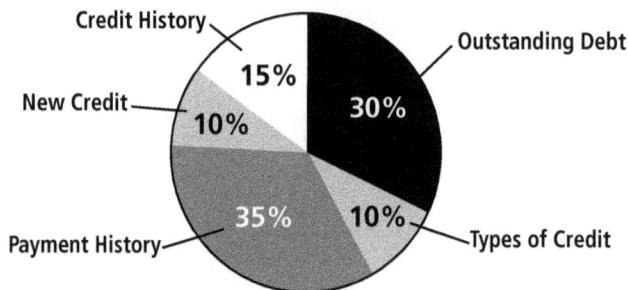

Credit History — 15%
Outstanding Debt — 30%
New Credit — 10%
Payment History — 35%
Types of Credit — 10%

Credit Inquiries

When applying for credit (i.e., credit card, auto loan, mortgage) lenders will review your credit report in order to make a decision about whether they should approve or deny your request. This is considered a hard credit inquiry.

Hard inquires occur when you've applied for credit and the lender reviews your credit report to determine your credit worthiness. A hard inquiry can potentially affect your credit scores if you allow lenders to pull your credit frequently in order to obtain a small discount towards a small purchase.

A soft inquiry occurs when you check your credit score, or a lender checks your credit score for a preapproval offer. Soft inquires do not impact your credit scores.

We will talk more about the types of companies that determine your credit score. For now, the higher the number, the better – the more credit worthy you are. The number is very important as you move through different times in your life.

The Different Credit Agencies

The Big Three

In the United States, there are three credit agencies (sometimes referred to as Credit Bureaus) that are used to keep track of a customer's repayment history data. These agencies are Equifax, Experian, and TransUnion.

These companies compete with one another for the ability to access your repayment history, update, and capture all of your purchasing information. The information that is retrieved is basically the same although there are slight differences.

Your credit score should **NEVER** be a mystery to you. You are entitled to a free complete copy (including creditor details) of your credit report every 12 months from these three credit agencies.

EQUIFAX

Equifax uses a base scale number ranging between 280-850. The higher your Equifax score, the better your credit profile will be as you're marked as a low risk for creditors. They are far more likely to lend to you if your score is high. The higher your credit score, the less you're looked at as a credit risk.

www.equifax.com
Based in Atlanta, GA

TRANSUNION

TransUnion is the smallest of The Big Three. However, this doesn't mean Transunion is not equally as important as the bigger two. TransUnion uses VantageScore to calculate your score, based on your credit and financial history. The VantageScore can range from 300-850.

www.transunion.com
Headquartered in Chicago, Illinois

EXPERIAN

The only one of the Big Three that is not headquartered in the United States, Experian is based in Dublin, Ireland. Though they are not based in America, Experian is a multi-national company that collects information from more than a billion people worldwide. This number includes over twenty-five million consumers and businesses in the US. Experian scores are based on a scale ranging from 300-850. With Experian, a score of 700 or above is considered good.

www.experian.com
Based in Dublin, Ireland

Checking Your Credit Report

Checking your credit score and credit report quarterly is vital to having healthy credit, but most people don't know the difference between the two. Your **credit score** is the three-digit number that represents how well you manage your credit, and your **credit report** is a statement with a record of your credit activity. It's vital to keep an eye on this report because the Federal Trade Commission (FTC) has reported that, on average, one in five people will have a mistake on their credit report. By getting in the habit of checking your credit report, you'll be able to catch any error that gets made and ensure it's fixed.

If you need to check your credit report, contact your bank or credit card company to see if they offer this service free of charge. Additionally, you can track your credit report by signing up for an online monitoring service like IdentityForce or CreditSesame, or going online to annualcreditreport.com.

Good vs. Bad Credit – It's Really Up to You

You are the only person who has control of your credit score. You control the credit you apply for and how you repay your loans. If you are irresponsible with your credit, your low credit score can control the interest rates and/or fees you pay when you purchase an item (laptop, cell phone, car, home, etc.). Good credit is not hard to achieve if you are responsible. However, a bad credit score can limit your financial goals and impact your financial decisions for seven years.

When it comes to accruing and maintaining good credit, making payments on time is critical! When you make your payments on time, this shows potential creditors that you are a trustworthy customer. However, late payments create derogatory (negative) marks on your credit report. Each derogatory mark that you receive lowers your credit score. Late payments reported to credit agencies can drop your score 50 points or more. This can impact you greatly, dropping a GREAT score down to GOOD and a GOOD score into the BAD score category. These problems will only be made worse if your late payments are sent to a collection agency. If the account is eventually forwarded to a collection agency, you will incur additional fees and the collection account will impact your score.

If the outstanding balance results in a negative mark on your credit report, that negative remark remains on your credit report for 7 years from the last payment activity date (i.e., the last date you made a payment on the account). YEARS. Truly let that sink in. We are not talking about a few weeks, or months. All it takes is one late payment to lower your score drastically for years into the future.

Impact of a Negative Credit Score

There is no way around it—having a low credit score is a headache that is extremely difficult to overcome. Not only will you need to pay outstanding balances that caused the negative marks (which now probably include multiple late fees, high interest rates, and fines), your low credit score also takes away many of your buying options.

The type of car you drive, the amount of money banks are willing to lend to you, and even the neighborhood and home you live in; all of these things can be impacted by a low credit score.

For example, let's compare the interest rate on a car loan for someone with good credit versus a person with a bad credit score.

Credit Score Ranges

350 to 500: Applicants will not likely be approved for credit.

500 to 600: Applicants may be approved for some credit; however, the interest rates may be unfavorable and require the applicant to make a large down payment.

601 to 660: Applicants may be approved for credit; however, the interest rate may be high.

661 to 780: Applicants likely to be approved for credit at competitive interest rates.

781 to 850: Applicants most likely to be approved and receive the best interest rates and most favorable loan terms. No down payment usually required.

High Credit Scores equals lower payments.

IMPACTS OF A HIGH CREDIT SCORE VERSUS LOW CREDIT SCORE		
Credit Score	**New Car Annual Percentage Rate**	**Loan Term**
750 & Higher	1.99 APR	5 years
749 to 699	2.99 APR	5 years
698 to 648	4.99 APR	5 years
647 to 597	6.99 APR	5 years
596 to 546	11.99 APR	5 years
546 & Lower	Loan Application Denied	N/A

For example, if you purchase a new car for $20,000 and your credit sore is 750 or higher, your monthly car pay amount is $350.47. If your credit score was 596, your monthly car payment amount is $444.79.

By having a higher credit score you save $94.32 a month! The estimated car payment was based on the APR listed in the chart above.

Having a high credit score can save you thousands of dollars by avoiding high interest rates, late fees, and penalties.

- Lower interest rates
- Avoid security deposits for apartments or loans
- The ability to purchase what you want from lenders (i.e., banks, credit unions, creditors) without paying a high interest rate or a deposit
- Lower interest rates when purchasing cell phones and other high-priced electronics (i.e., laptops, digital cameras)
- Lower monthly loan payments
- Easier to get approved for loans or line of credit
- Avoid security deposit for utilities (i.e., electronic, cable, water)

How Your Credit Score Can Impact Your Job

Did you know? Sometimes employers will also pull your credit report as a way to determine whether you'd be a reliable employee. That may seem well and good, but it can also have an adverse impact. Negative items (i.e., late payments, collection agencies) may be reported to all three of the major agencies. If you have several late payments reported to the credit agencies, the late payments will lower your credit score. The employer may take into consideration how responsible you may be as their employee.

- I will attain all the riches that I desire with time.

- I am on my way to becoming wealthy.

- Everything I need to build wealth is available to me right now.

- There is money all around me; I just have to grab it.

- I am a magnet that can attract money in any endeavor I undertake.

- I love attracting money.

- Money falls into my lap in miraculous ways.

- People love giving me money.

- I trust that more money is coming to me.

- I am aligned with the energy of wealth and abundance.

- I allow money to flow easily to me.

- Money is being drawn to me in every moment.

- An abundance of money is flowing into my life right now.

- Money is unlimited, and my prosperity is unlimited.

- Money is abundant, and I attract it naturally.

- Money is pouring into my life.

- I attract massive amounts of money to me.

PART TWO

Tips and Strategies to Achieve and Maintain Good Credit

Make It All Work Together for You

Protect your personal credit file

It's important to actively monitor your personal credit file at any age. Unfortunately, someone can steal your identity and purchase items or obtain a line of credit using your social security number.

- Don't just allow any creditor or lender to check your credit in order to obtain a small discount on a purchase.

- Safeguard your identify while online! Don't enter your personal information (i.e., date of birth, social security number, and home address) when browsing or surfing online.

- Every want is not a need. Make sure you can afford the goods (laptop, cell phone, automobile, etc.) or services before applying for a line of credit.

- You are the only person who has control of your credit score. You control the credit you apply for and how you repay your loans.

Your credit score is the most important number in your life; more important than the date you were born, graduate, or got married.

Credit Tips

- Apply for new credit only as needed
- Pay your bills on time
- Check your credit reports for errors
- Keep old credit cards open to maintain a longer credit history
- Make payments in full when possible, and otherwise pay at least the minimum
- If you're planning to take out a loan you should rate shop. Rate shopping allows you to determine which lender best meets your needs. For example, if you apply with several lenders within a 30-day timeframe it will only be considered as one inquiry.
- Live within your credit means and don't exceed your limit
- Consider using a credit monitoring service
- If you haven't established enough credit yet, try to raise your credit score by using credit boosting services

Credit Report Review Checklist

It is essential to review your credit report carefully once you receive one. There may be mistakes listed that could end up costing you. Use our checklist below to help you review your credit report.

Date _____ Name of Credit Agency _____

1. Does your name on the report match the name on your ID?
2. Is your social security number reported correctly?
3. Are both your phone number and address, correct?
4. Have you checked to see if there are previous addresses you need to correct?
5. Is your employment history reported correctly?
6. Have they listed your marital status correctly?
7. Have you verified that everything listed under personal information is correct?
8. Does anything in the personal information section need to be corrected?

Review this section carefully and note anything that is not correct.

9. Have you verified that the current balance is correct?
10. If you are an authorized or joint user on an account, is it listed?
11. If you have debts paid in full or balances discharged for bankruptcy, are they reported correctly?
12. Have you verified that all accounts you closed are listed as "closed by consumer"?
13. If you are a cosigner on a loan, is it correctly listed?
14. Are there negative items reported on your credit accounts? Are they reported correctly?

At this stage, also look for missed or late payments. Highlight anything you think is incorrect.

15. Are there any accounts that have been listed twice?
16. Is there any negative information listed in the report that has exceeded the reporting limit?

Negative information, including late payments, is reported at least seven years from the last date a payment was made on the account.

17. Do you have any reason to believe you have fallen victim to identity theft?

Credit Agency Contact Information

Experian
Online - https://www.experian.com/disputes/main.html

Please refer to the phone number provided on the credit report or on the website

Equifax
Online - https://www.equifax.com/personal/credit-report-services/credit-dispute/

Please refer to the phone number provided on the credit report or website

TransUnion
Online - https://www.transunion.com/credit-disputes/dispute-your-credit

Please refer to the phone number provided on the credit report or website

Filing a Dispute Checklist

If you noticed incorrect information on your credit report, you must report it to the credit agency that provided the report. Use our checklist below to file a dispute.

Date _____ Who are you sending the dispute to? _____

- Write a letter to the credit agency that provided the report. Make sure it includes:
  o The account number for the item you feel is incorrect.
  o If applicable, copies of bills that show you paid for each item on time.
  o Your mailing address and phone number in case the credit agency needs to reach out to you for more information.
- For each item you are disputing, be sure to explain in detail why you believe the report is incorrect.
- Make sure you record a copy of any dispute you send.
- Submit the dispute. Most agencies allow you to file a dispute on their website, but you can also submit a paper dispute through the mail if you wish.

Generally, credit agencies have 30-45 days to review your claim.

Debt Snowball Plan

Debt can be overwhelming, but you can get it under control with the Debt Snowball Plan. To understand this plan, you need to understand a snowball. When you're building a snowball, you start by packing snow into a tight ball, and it gets bigger while you roll it around in the snow. You take this same principle and apply it to your debt. Start with the smallest debt and pay this in full while making the minimum payments on the rest. Once this is paid off, move on to the next smallest debt and then so on until you're debt-free. The Debt Snowball Plan works because it requires you to change your habits and commit fully to paying down your debt.

- Pay debts in order of balance amount.
- Start by listing debt from the smallest to the largest.
- Make minimum payments on all debts except the smallest. If debts have the same balance, put the debt with the highest interest rate first.
- Focus on paying off one balance at a time. Pay as much as possible on your smallest debt.
- Repeat until each debt is paid in full.

52-Week $1 Saving Challenge

If you start with $1, you could turn that into $1,378 in just one year with this *52-Week $1 Saving Challenge*. To start this challenge, first determine where to put this savings. Instead of the piggy bank you've had since childhood, consider opening a high yield savings account to house your money. That way, your money will also be earning interest all year long.

Once you have your savings account set up, it's time to start your challenge. The first week you will deposit $1 into your savings account; the second week, you'll deposit $2; the third week, you'll deposit $3, and so on. You want to match your deposit to the number of the week you are on. For example, on week 33, you are depositing $33. If you stick to this plan, you'll have saved $1,378 in just one year, but don't let your momentum stop you there. Nothing is stopping you from starting the 52-Week $1 Saving Challenge all over again.

52-WEEK $ 1 SAVING CHALLENGE CHART

I AM SAVING FOR:

WK#	DATE	AMT	BAL	DONE	WK#	DATE	AMT	BAL	DONE
1		$1	$1		27		$27	$378	
2		$2	$3		28		$28	$396	
3		$3	$6		29		$29	$425	
4		$4	$10		30		$30	$455	
5		$5	$15		31		$31	$486	
6		$6	$21		32		$32	$518	
7		$7	$28		33		$33	$551	
8		$8	$36		34		$34	$595	
9		$9	$45		35		$35	$630	
10		$10	$55		36		$36	$666	
11		$11	$66		37		$37	$703	
12		$12	$78		38		$38	$741	
13		$13	$91		39		$39	$780	
14		$14	$105		40		$40	$820	
15		$15	$120		41		$41	$861	
16		$16	$136		42		$42	$903	
17		$17	$153		43		$43	$946	
18		$18	$171		44		$44	$990	
19		$19	$190		45		$45	$1,035	
20		$20	$210		46		$46	$1,081	
21		$21	$231		47		$47	$1,128	
22		$22	$253		48		$48	$1,176	
23		$23	$276		49		$49	$1,255	
24		$24	$300		50		$50	$1,275	
25		$25	$325		51		$51	$1,326	
26		$26	$351		53		$52	$1,378	

Credit Tips When Purchasing a House

Before purchasing a house, be sure to have:

- Copies of at least three tax returns
- Tax transcripts for the past three years
- The three most recent bank statements for all your accounts
- The last three copies of your employer pay statements
- 5% to 6% of the total purchase price saved for the closing costs
- At least 3% of the total purchase price saved for the down payment (if not, look for a seller who helps with down payment assistance)
- A copy of your SSN card and valid ID

In addition to having the above items, you need to remember to:

- Pay all bills on time.
- Pay off collections or liens – be sure to keep the receipts showing they are paid off.
- Inquire about first-time buyers' grants for your city or state.
- Keep your debt-to-income ratio (DTI) low.
- Respond to inquiries from your lender as soon as possible.

Make sure you don't:

- Apply for a new credit card until your loan closes, and the loan money has been disbursed
- Cosign for any new credit while going through the process of buying property

Another important thing to consider is if someone is gifting you money towards the purchase of property, you need to make sure they are prepared to show bank statements for the last two months.

Additionally, you will need three months of pay stubs for any additional part-time jobs you work. If you own a business, make sure you have an itemized list of all business expenses, and you are filing your tax returns correctly. Be prepared to show your tax returns for the past three years.

While in the process of purchasing a home, you may come across the term "underwriting." Underwriting is when a lender verifies your income, debt, assets, and details of the property to give final approval on your loan. While you probably won't work with an underwriter directly, it's important to understand what they are and do. For instance, underwriting might be the reason your lender is asking you for additional documents about your finances. Responding to your lender quickly ensures the underwriter can do their job, and your loan can be finalized faster.

PART THREE

Time to take action!

Creating your Goals

Tracking Your Monthly Expenses and Quarterly Credit

How to Set Up Your Goals Each Month

The first step in setting up your financial goals is to understand what they are. Goals can be both long-term and short-term. For example, your long-term goal might be to save enough for retirement, while your short-term goal is to have $5,000 saved.

Monthly goals are considered short-term goals. The first step to setting up your monthly goals is to sit down at the first of each month and assess your finances. When deciding on your goal for that month, make it specific and measurable. Then write it down. A goal that is too vague or not measurable is, "I want to be better at saving money." If this was your goal, there is no way for you to track it, resulting in losing motivation.

Use the pages at the beginning of each month in this planner to answer the questions to set and track your goals.

**USE THE SPACE ON THE THE FOLLOWING PAGES
TO ANSWER THE QUESTIONS**

MONTHLY GOALS

1. Write down your goals.
2. Make sure that you are specific about your goals.
3. Select the date you would like to have these goals completed.
4. What is the "why" for these goals?
5. Make sure your goals are measurable.
6. Create a MAP for your goals. **(Massive Action Plan)**
7. Monitor and track your progress.

USE THE SPACE BELOW AND THE FOLLOWING PAGES TO ANSWER THE QUESTIONS

Develop fiscal management skills. (Next 3 months)

Spend more time with family and friends. (Next 3 months)

Advance in my career. (Next 12 months)

Increase my income by 10% within the next 12 months.

Learn how to manage my time better. (Next 3 months)

Give back to my community in ways that matter to me. (Next 12 months)

Save $5000 per year. (Next 12 months)

Strive for home ownership. (Next 6 months)

Start Emergency Fund. (Next 6 months)

Pay off debt. (Within the next 2 to 5 years)

Save for retirement. (Within the next 5 to 10 years)

• Make sure your goals can be measured. Although, it is good to set a high goal, make sure your goals are attainable.

Develop fiscal management skills. (Next 3 months)

Spend more time with family and friends. (Next 3 months)

Learn how to manage my time better. (Next 3 months)

_____

_____

_____

_____

_____

_____

_____

_____

_____

_____

_____

_____

Calendar Sample

Please enter the month date in each block. For example, first block please enter 1 and the appropriate date in the remaining blocks.

MONTH: January

1	2	3	4
5	6 Order Free Credit Report	7	8 Review Free Credit Report for accuracy.
9	10	11	12
13 Received Bi-weekly Pay Check	14	15	16
17 ABC Credit Card Payment Due	18	19	20

20 23 _____

21	22	23
24 Automobile Payment Due	25	26
27 Received Bi-weekly Pay Check	28	29
30	31	

Personal Goals

Develop fiscal management skills.

_____

Spend more time with family and friends.

_____

Advance in my career.

_____

_____

Financial Goals

Save $5000 per year.

Strive for home ownership.

Start Emergency Fund.

Pay off debt.

Save for retirement.

_____

_____

_____

Tracking Monthly Expenses

Everyone tells you it's important to track your monthly expenses, but they don't tell you why. The answer is simple – it keeps you accountable. Tracking your monthly expenses is the best way to ensure you're sticking to your budget and also allows you to find any areas you can cut back on your spending.

Let's say you're reviewing your monthly expenses and see you spend about $200 a month on having food delivered. You compare this to the amount you budget for groceries and find you can cut back on the food delivery. Furthermore, this $200 you're saving on food delivery could be applied towards your Debt Snowball Plan.

The first step to tracking your finances is to create a budget. If you've never made a budget before, it's a monthly plan of what you will be doing with your money – ensuring you have enough for all your bills and necessities. Next, you need to be tracking all the money you make and all the money you spend. After you have everything tracked, review your expenses and see if there are any adjustments you need to make to your spending habits.

INCOME	BUDGET	ACTUAL	DIFFERENCE
Salary	$39,000	$39,000	0
Gifts recieved	0	0	0
Refunds	0	0	0
Transfer from Savings	0	$700	0
Other Income	0	0	0
TOTAL INCOME	$39,700	$39,700	0

SAVINGS	BUDGET	ACTUAL	DIFFERENCE
Emergency Fund	$1,000	$700	$300
Holiday	$500	$400	$100
Investments	$200	$150	$50
Education Fund	0	0	0
Travel	$800	$650	$150
Other Savings			
TOTAL SAVINGS	$2,500	$1,900	$600

EXPENSES	BUDGET	ACTUAL	DIFFERENCE
Mortgage/Rent Payment	$1200.00	$1200.00	0
Home/Rental Insurance			
Auto Payment	$650.00	$600.00	$50.00
Groceries	$400.00	$375.00	$25.00
Utilities	$600.00	$500.00	$100.00
Cell Phone	$250.00	$250.00	0
Cable/Internet	$180.00	$180.00	0
Personal hygiene Items	$125.00	$100.00	$25.00
Pets	$75.00	$70.00	0
Entertainment/Recreation	$200.00	$175.00	$25.00
Clothing	$100.00	$50.00	$50.00
Dry Cleaning	$50.00	$30.00	$20.00
Health Insurance	$125.00	$125.00	0
Life Insurance	$85.00	$85.00	0
Home Appliance Warranty	$50.00	$50.00	0
Donations	$50.00	$50.00	0
Membership/Subscription	$60.00	$60.00	0
Daycare	$400.00	$375.00	$25.00
Credit Card Payments (Exclude previous expenses recorded in a specific category)	$300.00	$275.00	$25.00
Emergency Fund	$1000.00	$900.00	$100.00
Travel	$800.00	$750.00	$50.00
Vacation	$1000.00	$800.00	$200.00
Student Loan	$125.00	$115.00	$10.00
Gifts	$50.00	$40.00	$10.00
Fun Money	$150.00	$125.00	$25.00

Creditor Tracker Description

The Creditor Tracker is a great tool to help you keep track of your credit card balances and maintain peak financial health. The Creditor Tracker is especially great if you feel overwhelmed while looking at your credit report. It's easy to break up all that information when using the Creditor Tracker because there is a designated slot for you to put who the creditor is, the balance on the account, how much the interest rate is, and your monthly payment. By putting all this information into the Creditor Tracker, you can quickly see this information. Even better, after a few months, you can see if there are any patterns with your credit. The Creditor Tracker will allow you to identify if your credit balance is getting too high or if your monthly payments are getting increasingly more expensive. The Creditor Tracker also lets you quickly see which of your credit cards has the highest or lowest interest rate, which can help you identify which account to tackle first if you're planning on applying the Debt Snowball plan. Be sure to include the Creditor Tracker in your monthly credit report review.

CREDITORS TRACKER

CREDIT'S NAME	MONTHLY PAYMENT	INTEREST RATE	BALANCE
ABC Credit Card	$100.00	6%	$4500.00
DEF Automobile Cooperation	$525.00	8%	$24,700.00

Quarterly Credit Score Check-In

In order to maintain good financial health, you need to check your credit report quarterly. A credit report is a statement with your credit information and activity. Checking your credit report quarterly is important because sometimes there are mistakes on your report. If you don't catch them, they could do harm to your credit. You can sign up for the credit reporting companies to get your credit report monthly. When you sit down to review your credit report, use our credit report review checklist to make sure you don't miss anything. If you notice something is wrong, check out our instructions to file a dispute before it harms your credit.

QUARTERLY CREDIT SCORE CHECK IN

MONTH 1 CREDIT SCORE:

620

MONTH 2 CREDIT SCORE:

640

What factors caused my credit score to increase or decrease?

P: Paid my creditors on time during months 1, 2 and 3.

C: Credit usage: The bonus allowed me to pay an extra $500 towards my credit card

L:

M:

R:

MONTH 3 CREDIT SCORE:

680

LEGEND:

P: Payment History
C: Credit Usage
L: Length of Credit
M: Mix of Credit
R: Recent Credit

MONTH ONE

1. Write down your goals.
2. Make sure that you are specific about your goals.
3. Select the date you would like to have these goals completed.
4. What is the "why" for these goals?
5. Make sure your goals are measurable.
6. Create a MAP for your goals. **(Massive Action Plan)**
7. Monitor and track your progress.

> **USE THE SPACE BELOW AND THE FOLLOWING PAGES TO ANSWER THE QUESTIONS**

_____

_____

_____

_____

_____

_____

_____

_____

_____

THIS MONTH'S GOALS

_____

_____

_____

_____

_____

_____

_____

_____

_____

_____

_____

_____

_____

_____

_____

_____

I attract money to me easily and effortlessly.

MONTH: _____

SUNDAY	MONDAY	TUESDAY	WEDNESDAY

20 _____

THURSDAY	FRIDAY	SATURDAY

Personal Goals

_____
_____
_____
_____
_____
_____

Financial Goals

_____
_____
_____
_____
_____
_____
_____

INCOME	BUDGET	ACTUAL	DIFFERENCE
Salary			
Gifts recieved			
Refunds			
Transfer from Savings			
Other Income			
TOTAL INCOME			

SAVINGS	BUDGET	ACTUAL	DIFFERENCE
Emergency Fund			
Holiday			
Investments			
Education Fund			
Travel			
Other Savings			
TOTAL SAVINGS			

MONTHLY BUDGET TRACKER

EXPENSES	BUDGET	ACTUAL	DIFFERENCE
Mortgage/Rent Payment			
Home/Rental Insurance			
Auto Payment			
Groceries			
Utilities			
Cell Phone			
Cable/Internet			
Personal hygiene Items			
Pets			
Entertainment/Recreation			
Clothing			
Dry Cleaning			
Health Insurance			
Life Insurance			
Home Appliance Warranty			
Donations			
Membership/Subscription			
Daycare			
Credit Card Payments (Exclude previous expenses recorded in a specific category)			
Emergency Fund			
Travel			
Vacation			
Student Loan			
Gifts			
Fun Money			

Creditors Tracker

The Creditor Tracker is a great tool to help you keep track of your credit card balances and maintain peak financial health. The Creditor Tracker is especially valuable if you feel overwhelmed while looking at your credit report. It's easy to break up all that information when using the Creditor Tracker because there is a designated slot for you to put who the creditor is, the balance on the account, how much the interest rate is, and your monthly payment. By putting all this information into the Creditor Tracker, you can quickly see this information. Even better, after a few months, you can see if there are any patterns with your credit.

The Creditor Tracker will allow you to identify if your credit balance is getting too high or if your monthly payments are getting increasingly more expensive. The Creditor Tracker also lets you quickly see which of your credit cards has the highest or lowest interest rate, which can help you identify which account to tackle first if you're planning on applying the Debt Snowball Plan. Be sure to include the Creditor Tracker in your monthly credit report review.

CREDITORS TRACKER

CREDIT'S NAME	MONTHLY PAYMENT	INTEREST RATE	BALANCE

MONTH TWO

1. Write down your goals.
2. Make sure that you are specific about your goals.
3. Select the date you would like to have these goals completed.
4. What is the "why" for these goals?
5. Make sure your goals are measurable.
6. Create a MAP for your goals. **(Massive Action Plan)**
7. Monitor and track your progress.

> ## USE THE SPACE BELOW AND THE FOLLOWING PAGES TO ANSWER THE QUESTIONS

_____

_____

_____

_____

_____

_____

_____

_____

THIS MONTH'S GOALS

THIS MONTH'S GOALS

_____

_____

_____

_____

_____

_____

_____

_____

_____

_____

_____

_____

_____

_____

_____

_____

Everything I need to build wealth is available to me right now..

MONTH: _____

20 _____

Personal
Goals

_____
_____
_____
_____
_____
_____
_____

Financial
Goals

_____
_____
_____
_____
_____
_____
_____

INCOME	BUDGET	ACTUAL	DIFFERENCE
Salary			
Gifts recieved			
Refunds			
Transfer from Savings			
Other Income			
TOTAL INCOME			

SAVINGS	BUDGET	ACTUAL	DIFFERENCE
Emergency Fund			
Holiday			
Investments			
Education Fund			
Travel			
Other Savings			
TOTAL SAVINGS			

EXPENSES	BUDGET	ACTUAL	DIFFERENCE
Mortgage/Rent Payment			
Home/Rental Insurance			
Auto Payment			
Groceries			
Utilities			
Cell Phone			
Cable/Internet			
Personal hygiene Items			
Pets			
Entertainment/Recreation			
Clothing			
Dry Cleaning			
Health Insurance			
Life Insurance			
Home Appliance Warranty			
Donations			
Membership/Subscription			
Daycare			
Credit Card Payments (Exclude previous expenses recorded in a specific category)			
Emergency Fund			
Travel			
Vacation			
Student Loan			
Gifts			
Fun Money			

MONTHLY BUDGET TRACKER

Creditors Tracker

The Creditor Tracker is a great tool to help you keep track of your credit card balances and maintain peak financial health. The Creditor Tracker is especially valuable if you feel overwhelmed while looking at your credit report. It's easy to break up all that information when using the Creditor Tracker because there is a designated slot for you to put who the creditor is, the balance on the account, how much the interest rate is, and your monthly payment. By putting all this information into the Creditor Tracker, you can quickly see this information. Even better, after a few months, you can see if there are any patterns with your credit.

The Creditor Tracker will allow you to identify if your credit balance is getting too high or if your monthly payments are getting increasingly more expensive. The Creditor Tracker also lets you quickly see which of your credit cards has the highest or lowest interest rate, which can help you identify which account to tackle first if you're planning on applying the Debt Snowball Plan. Be sure to include the Creditor Tracker in your monthly credit report review.

CREDITORS TRACKER

CREDITORS	BALANCE	INTEREST RATE	MONTHLY PAYMENT

MONTH THREE

1. Write down your goals.
2. Make sure that you are specific about your goals.
3. Select the date you would like to have these goals completed.
4. What is the "why" for these goals?
5. Make sure your goals are measurable.
6. Create a MAP for your goals. **(Massive Action Plan)**
7. Monitor and track your progress.

USE THE SPACE BELOW AND THE FOLLOWING PAGES TO ANSWER THE QUESTIONS

_____

_____

_____

_____

_____

_____

_____

_____

THIS MONTH'S GOALS

_____

_____

_____

_____

_____

_____

_____

_____

_____

_____

_____

_____

_____

_____

_____

_____

I am a magnet that can attract money in any endeavor I undertake.

MONTH: _____

20 _____

Personal
Goals

_____
_____
_____
_____
_____
_____

Financial
Goals

_____
_____
_____
_____
_____
_____
_____

INCOME	BUDGET	ACTUAL	DIFFERENCE
Salary			
Gifts recieved			
Refunds			
Transfer from Savings			
Other Income			
TOTAL INCOME			

SAVINGS	BUDGET	ACTUAL	DIFFERENCE
Emergency Fund			
Holiday			
Investments			
Education Fund			
Travel			
Other Savings			
TOTAL SAVINGS			

EXPENSES	BUDGET	ACTUAL	DIFFERENCE
Mortgage/Rent Payment			
Home/Rental Insurance			
Auto Payment			
Groceries			
Utilities			
Cell Phone			
Cable/Internet			
Personal hygiene Items			
Pets			
Entertainment/Recreation			
Clothing			
Dry Cleaning			
Health Insurance			
Life Insurance			
Home Appliance Warranty			
Donations			
Membership/Subscription			
Daycare			
Credit Card Payments (Exclude previous expenses recorded in a specific category)			
Emergency Fund			
Travel			
Vacation			
Student Loan			
Gifts			
Fun Money			

MONTHLY BUDGET TRACKER

MONTH THREE

69

Creditors Tracker

The Creditor Tracker is a great tool to help you keep track of your credit card balances and maintain peak financial health. The Creditor Tracker is especially valuable if you feel overwhelmed while looking at your credit report. It's easy to break up all that information when using the Creditor Tracker because there is a designated slot for you to put who the creditor is, the balance on the account, how much the interest rate is, and your monthly payment. By putting all this information into the Creditor Tracker, you can quickly see this information. Even better, after a few months, you can see if there are any patterns with your credit.

The Creditor Tracker will allow you to identify if your credit balance is getting too high or if your monthly payments are getting increasingly more expensive. The Creditor Tracker also lets you quickly see which of your credit cards has the highest or lowest interest rate, which can help you identify which account to tackle first if you're planning on applying the Debt Snowball Plan. Be sure to include the Creditor Tracker in your monthly credit report review.

CREDITORS TRACKER

NOTES

QUARTERLY CREDIT SCORE CHECK IN

MONTH 1 CREDIT SCORE:

What factors caused my credit score to increase or decrease?

P: _____

MONTH 2 CREDIT SCORE:

C: _____

L: _____

M: _____

R: _____

MONTH 3 CREDIT SCORE:

LEGEND:
   P: Payment History
   C: Credit Usage
   L: Length of Credit
   M: Mix of Credit
   R: Recent Credit

MONTH FOUR

1. Write down your goals.
2. Make sure that you are specific about your goals.
3. Select the date you would like to have these goals completed.
4. What is the "why" for these goals?
5. Make sure your goals are measurable.
6. Create a MAP for your goals. **(Massive Action Plan)**
7. Monitor and track your progress.

USE THE SPACE BELOW AND THE FOLLOWING PAGES TO ANSWER THE QUESTIONS

_____

_____

_____

_____

_____

_____

_____

_____

_____

_____

_____

_____

_____

_____

_____

_____

_____

_____

_____

_____

_____

_____

_____

I trust that more money is coming to me.

MONTH: _____

20 _____

Personal
Goals

_____
_____
_____
_____
_____
_____

Financial
Goals

_____
_____
_____
_____
_____
_____
_____
_____

INCOME	BUDGET	ACTUAL	DIFFERENCE
Salary			
Gifts recieved			
Refunds			
Transfer from Savings			
Other Income			
TOTAL INCOME			

SAVINGS	BUDGET	ACTUAL	DIFFERENCE
Emergency Fund			
Holiday			
Investments			
Education Fund			
Travel			
Other Savings			
TOTAL SAVINGS			

EXPENSES	BUDGET	ACTUAL	DIFFERENCE
Mortgage/Rent Payment			
Home/Rental Insurance			
Auto Payment			
Groceries			
Utilities			
Cell Phone			
Cable/Internet			
Personal hygiene Items			
Pets			
Entertainment/Recreation			
Clothing			
Dry Cleaning			
Health Insurance			
Life Insurance			
Home Appliance Warranty			
Donations			
Membership/Subscription			
Daycare			
Credit Card Payments (Exclude previous expenses recorded in a specific category)			
Emergency Fund			
Travel			
Vacation			
Student Loan			
Gifts			
Fun Money			

Creditors Tracker

The Creditor Tracker is a great tool to help you keep track of your credit card balances and maintain peak financial health. The Creditor Tracker is especially valuable if you feel overwhelmed while looking at your credit report. It's easy to break up all that information when using the Creditor Tracker because there is a designated slot for you to put who the creditor is, the balance on the account, how much the interest rate is, and your monthly payment. By putting all this information into the Creditor Tracker, you can quickly see this information. Even better, after a few months, you can see if there are any patterns with your credit.

The Creditor Tracker will allow you to identify if your credit balance is getting too high or if your monthly payments are getting increasingly more expensive. The Creditor Tracker also lets you quickly see which of your credit cards has the highest or lowest interest rate, which can help you identify which account to tackle first if you're planning on applying the Debt Snowball Plan. Be sure to include the Creditor Tracker in your monthly credit report review.

CREDITORS TRACKER

MONTH FIVE

1. Write down your goals.
2. Make sure that you are specific about your goals.
3. Select the date you would like to have these goals completed.
4. What is the "why" for these goals?
5. Make sure your goals are measurable.
6. Create a MAP for your goals. **(Massive Action Plan)**
7. Monitor and track your progress.

USE THE SPACE BELOW AND THE FOLLOWING PAGES TO ANSWER THE QUESTIONS

_____

_____

_____

_____

_____

_____

_____

_____

_____

_____

_____

_____

_____

_____

_____

_____

_____

_____

_____

_____

_____

_____

_____

_____

THIS MONTH'S GOALS

MONTH FIVE

I release all resistance to attracting money.

MONTH: _____

20 _____

Personal
Goals

_____
_____
_____
_____
_____
_____

Financial
Goals

_____
_____
_____
_____
_____
_____
_____
_____

INCOME	BUDGET	ACTUAL	DIFFERENCE
Salary			
Gifts recieved			
Refunds			
Transfer from Savings			
Other Income			
TOTAL INCOME			

SAVINGS	BUDGET	ACTUAL	DIFFERENCE
Emergency Fund			
Holiday			
Investments			
Education Fund			
Travel			
Other Savings			
TOTAL SAVINGS			

EXPENSES	BUDGET	ACTUAL	DIFFERENCE
Mortgage/Rent Payment			
Home/Rental Insurance			
Auto Payment			
Groceries			
Utilities			
Cell Phone			
Cable/Internet			
Personal hygiene Items			
Pets			
Entertainment/Recreation			
Clothing			
Dry Cleaning			
Health Insurance			
Life Insurance			
Home Appliance Warranty			
Donations			
Membership/Subscription			
Daycare			
Credit Card Payments (Exclude previous expenses recorded in a specific category)			
Emergency Fund			
Travel			
Vacation			
Student Loan			
Gifts			
Fun Money			

Creditors Tracker

The Creditor Tracker is a great tool to help you keep track of your credit card balances and maintain peak financial health. The Creditor Tracker is especially valuable if you feel overwhelmed while looking at your credit report. It's easy to break up all that information when using the Creditor Tracker because there is a designated slot for you to put who the creditor is, the balance on the account, how much the interest rate is, and your monthly payment. By putting all this information into the Creditor Tracker, you can quickly see this information. Even better, after a few months, you can see if there are any patterns with your credit.

The Creditor Tracker will allow you to identify if your credit balance is getting too high or if your monthly payments are getting increasingly more expensive. The Creditor Tracker also lets you quickly see which of your credit cards has the highest or lowest interest rate, which can help you identify which account to tackle first if you're planning on applying the Debt Snowball Plan. Be sure to include the Creditor Tracker in your monthly credit report review.

CREDITORS TRACKER

MONTH SIX

1. Write down your goals.
2. Make sure that you are specific about your goals.
3. Select the date you would like to have these goals completed.
4. What is the "why" for these goals?
5. Make sure your goals are measurable.
6. Create a MAP for your goals. **(Massive Action Plan)**
7. Monitor and track your progress.

USE THE SPACE BELOW AND THE FOLLOWING PAGES TO ANSWER THE QUESTIONS

_____

_____

_____

_____

_____

_____

_____

_____

_____

_____

_____

_____

_____

_____

_____

_____

_____

_____

_____

_____

_____

_____

_____

I am aligned with the energy of wealth and abundance.

MONTH: _____

20 _____

Personal Goals

_____
_____
_____
_____
_____
_____
_____

Financial Goals

_____
_____
_____
_____
_____
_____
_____
_____

INCOME	BUDGET	ACTUAL	DIFFERENCE
Salary			
Gifts recieved			
Refunds			
Transfer from Savings			
Other Income			
TOTAL INCOME			

SAVINGS	BUDGET	ACTUAL	DIFFERENCE
Emergency Fund			
Holiday			
Investments			
Education Fund			
Travel			
Other Savings			
TOTAL SAVINGS			

EXPENSES	BUDGET	ACTUAL	DIFFERENCE
Mortgage/Rent Payment			
Home/Rental Insurance			
Auto Payment			
Groceries			
Utilities			
Cell Phone			
Cable/Internet			
Personal hygiene Items			
Pets			
Entertainment/Recreation			
Clothing			
Dry Cleaning			
Health Insurance			
Life Insurance			
Home Appliance Warranty			
Donations			
Membership/Subscription			
Daycare			
Credit Card Payments (Exclude previous expenses recorded in a specific category)			
Emergency Fund			
Travel			
Vacation			
Student Loan			
Gifts			
Fun Money			

Creditors Tracker

The Creditor Tracker is a great tool to help you keep track of your credit card balances and maintain peak financial health. The Creditor Tracker is especially valuable if you feel overwhelmed while looking at your credit report. It's easy to break up all that information when using the Creditor Tracker because there is a designated slot for you to put who the creditor is, the balance on the account, how much the interest rate is, and your monthly payment. By putting all this information into the Creditor Tracker, you can quickly see this information. Even better, after a few months, you can see if there are any patterns with your credit.

The Creditor Tracker will allow you to identify if your credit balance is getting too high or if your monthly payments are getting increasingly more expensive. The Creditor Tracker also lets you quickly see which of your credit cards has the highest or lowest interest rate, which can help you identify which account to tackle first if you're planning on applying the Debt Snowball Plan. Be sure to include the Creditor Tracker in your monthly credit report review.

CREDITORS TRACKER

NOTES

QUARTERLY CREDIT
SCORE CHECK IN

MONTH 4 CREDIT SCORE:

What factors caused my credit
score to increase or decrease?

MONTH 5 CREDIT SCORE:

P: _____

C: _____

L: _____

M: _____

R: _____

MONTH 6 CREDIT SCORE:

LEGEND:
P: Payment History
C: Credit Usage
L: Length of Credit
M: Mix of Credit
R: Recent Credit

MONTH SEVEN

1. Write down your goals.
2. Make sure that you are specific about your goals.
3. Select the date you would like to have these goals completed.
4. What is the "why" for these goals?
5. Make sure your goals are measurable.
6. Create a MAP for your goals. **(Massive Action Plan)**
7. Monitor and track your progress.

> **USE THE SPACE BELOW AND THE FOLLOWING PAGES TO ANSWER THE QUESTIONS**

THIS MONTH'S GOALS

_____

_____

_____

_____

_____

_____

_____

_____

_____

_____

_____

_____

_____

_____

Money is energy, and it flows into my life constantly.

MONTH: _____

20 _____

Personal
Goals

_____
_____
_____
_____
_____
_____

Financial
Goals

_____
_____
_____
_____
_____
_____
_____

INCOME	BUDGET	ACTUAL	DIFFERENCE
Salary			
Gifts recieved			
Refunds			
Transfer from Savings			
Other Income			
TOTAL INCOME			

SAVINGS	BUDGET	ACTUAL	DIFFERENCE
Emergency Fund			
Holiday			
Investments			
Education Fund			
Travel			
Other Savings			
TOTAL SAVINGS			

MONTHLY BUDGET TRACKER

EXPENSES	BUDGET	ACTUAL	DIFFERENCE
Mortgage/Rent Payment			
Home/Rental Insurance			
Auto Payment			
Groceries			
Utilities			
Cell Phone			
Cable/Internet			
Personal hygiene Items			
Pets			
Entertainment/Recreation			
Clothing			
Dry Cleaning			
Health Insurance			
Life Insurance			
Home Appliance Warranty			
Donations			
Membership/Subscription			
Daycare			
Credit Card Payments (Exclude previous expenses recorded in a specific category)			
Emergency Fund			
Travel			
Vacation			
Student Loan			
Gifts			
Fun Money			

Creditors Tracker

The Creditor Tracker is a great tool to help you keep track of your credit card balances and maintain peak financial health. The Creditor Tracker is especially valuable if you feel overwhelmed while looking at your credit report. It's easy to break up all that information when using the Creditor Tracker because there is a designated slot for you to put who the creditor is, the balance on the account, how much the interest rate is, and your monthly payment. By putting all this information into the Creditor Tracker, you can quickly see this information. Even better, after a few months, you can see if there are any patterns with your credit.

The Creditor Tracker will allow you to identify if your credit balance is getting too high or if your monthly payments are getting increasingly more expensive. The Creditor Tracker also lets you quickly see which of your credit cards has the highest or lowest interest rate, which can help you identify which account to tackle first if you're planning on applying the Debt Snowball Plan. Be sure to include the Creditor Tracker in your monthly credit report review.

CREDITORS TRACKER

MONTH EIGHT

1. Write down your goals.
2. Make sure that you are specific about your goals.
3. Select the date you would like to have these goals completed.
4. What is the "why" for these goals?
5. Make sure your goals are measurable.
6. Create a MAP for your goals. **(Massive Action Plan)**
7. Monitor and track your progress.

USE THE SPACE BELOW AND THE FOLLOWING PAGES TO ANSWER THE QUESTIONS

_____

_____

_____

_____

_____

_____

_____

_____

_____

THIS MONTH'S GOALS

THIS MONTH'S GOALS

_____

_____

_____

_____

_____

_____

_____

_____

_____

_____

_____

_____

_____

_____

_____

_____

I am so grateful for the ability to manifest money when I want it.

MONTH: _____

20 _____

Personal Goals

_____
_____
_____
_____
_____
_____

Financial Goals

_____
_____
_____
_____
_____
_____
_____

INCOME	BUDGET	ACTUAL	DIFFERENCE
Salary			
Gifts recieved			
Refunds			
Transfer from Savings			
Other Income			
TOTAL INCOME			

SAVINGS	BUDGET	ACTUAL	DIFFERENCE
Emergency Fund			
Holiday			
Investments			
Education Fund			
Travel			
Other Savings			
TOTAL SAVINGS			

EXPENSES	BUDGET	ACTUAL	DIFFERENCE
Mortgage/Rent Payment			
Home/Rental Insurance			
Auto Payment			
Groceries			
Utilities			
Cell Phone			
Cable/Internet			
Personal hygiene Items			
Pets			
Entertainment/Recreation			
Clothing			
Dry Cleaning			
Health Insurance			
Life Insurance			
Home Appliance Warranty			
Donations			
Membership/Subscription			
Daycare			
Credit Card Payments (Exclude previous expenses recorded in a specific category)			
Emergency Fund			
Travel			
Vacation			
Student Loan			
Gifts			
Fun Money			

MONTHLY BUDGET TRACKER

Creditors Tracker

The Creditor Tracker is a great tool to help you keep track of your credit card balances and maintain peak financial health. The Creditor Tracker is especially valuable if you feel overwhelmed while looking at your credit report. It's easy to break up all that information when using the Creditor Tracker because there is a designated slot for you to put who the creditor is, the balance on the account, how much the interest rate is, and your monthly payment. By putting all this information into the Creditor Tracker, you can quickly see this information. Even better, after a few months, you can see if there are any patterns with your credit.

The Creditor Tracker will allow you to identify if your credit balance is getting too high or if your monthly payments are getting increasingly more expensive. The Creditor Tracker also lets you quickly see which of your credit cards has the highest or lowest interest rate, which can help you identify which account to tackle first if you're planning on applying the Debt Snowball Plan. Be sure to include the Creditor Tracker in your monthly credit report review.

CREDITORS TRACKER

MONTH NINE

1. Write down your goals.
2. Make sure that you are specific about your goals.
3. Select the date you would like to have these goals completed.
4. What is the "why" for these goals?
5. Make sure your goals are measurable.
6. Create a MAP for your goals. **(Massive Action Plan)**
7. Monitor and track your progress.

USE THE SPACE BELOW AND THE FOLLOWING PAGES TO ANSWER THE QUESTIONS

_____

_____

_____

_____

_____

_____

_____

_____

_____

THIS MONTH'S GOALS

THIS MONTH'S GOALS

_____

_____

_____

_____

_____

_____

_____

_____

_____

_____

_____

_____

_____

_____

I have the power to attract wealth and money into my life.

MONTH: _____

20 _____

Personal
Goals

_____
_____
_____
_____
_____
_____
_____

Financial
Goals

_____
_____
_____
_____
_____
_____
_____
_____
_____

INCOME	BUDGET	ACTUAL	DIFFERENCE
Salary			
Gifts recieved			
Refunds			
Transfer from Savings			
Other Income			
TOTAL INCOME			

SAVINGS	BUDGET	ACTUAL	DIFFERENCE
Emergency Fund			
Holiday			
Investments			
Education Fund			
Travel			
Other Savings			
TOTAL SAVINGS			

EXPENSES	BUDGET	ACTUAL	DIFFERENCE
Mortgage/Rent Payment			
Home/Rental Insurance			
Auto Payment			
Groceries			
Utilities			
Cell Phone			
Cable/Internet			
Personal hygiene Items			
Pets			
Entertainment/Recreation			
Clothing			
Dry Cleaning			
Health Insurance			
Life Insurance			
Home Appliance Warranty			
Donations			
Membership/Subscription			
Daycare			
Credit Card Payments (Exclude previous expenses recorded in a specific category)			
Emergency Fund			
Travel			
Vacation			
Student Loan			
Gifts			
Fun Money			

Creditors Tracker

The Creditor Tracker is a great tool to help you keep track of your credit card balances and maintain peak financial health. The Creditor Tracker is especially valuable if you feel overwhelmed while looking at your credit report. It's easy to break up all that information when using the Creditor Tracker because there is a designated slot for you to put who the creditor is, the balance on the account, how much the interest rate is, and your monthly payment. By putting all this information into the Creditor Tracker, you can quickly see this information. Even better, after a few months, you can see if there are any patterns with your credit.

The Creditor Tracker will allow you to identify if your credit balance is getting too high or if your monthly payments are getting increasingly more expensive. The Creditor Tracker also lets you quickly see which of your credit cards has the highest or lowest interest rate, which can help you identify which account to tackle first if you're planning on applying the Debt Snowball Plan. Be sure to include the Creditor Tracker in your monthly credit report review.

CREDITORS TRACKER

NOTES

QUARTERLY CREDIT SCORE CHECK IN

MONTH 7 CREDIT SCORE:

What factors caused my credit score to increase or decrease?

MONTH 8 CREDIT SCORE:

P: _____

C: _____

L: _____

M: _____

R: _____

MONTH 9 CREDIT SCORE:

LEGEND:

P: Payment History

C: Credit Usage

L: Length of Credit

M: Mix of Credit

R: Recent Credit

MONTH TEN

1. Write down your goals.
2. Make sure that you are specific about your goals.
3. Select the date you would like to have these goals completed.
4. What is the "why" for these goals?
5. Make sure your goals are measurable.
6. Create a MAP for your goals. **(Massive Action Plan)**
7. Monitor and track your progress.

> **USE THE SPACE BELOW AND THE FOLLOWING PAGES TO ANSWER THE QUESTIONS**

_____

_____

_____

_____

_____

_____

_____

_____

_____

_____

_____

_____

_____

_____

_____

_____

_____

_____

_____

_____

_____

_____

_____

_____

Money is unlimited, and my prosperity is unlimited.

MONTH: _____

20 _____

Personal Goals

_____
_____
_____
_____
_____
_____

Financial Goals

_____
_____
_____
_____
_____
_____
_____
_____

INCOME	BUDGET	ACTUAL	DIFFERENCE
Salary			
Gifts recieved			
Refunds			
Transfer from Savings			
Other Income			
TOTAL INCOME			

SAVINGS	BUDGET	ACTUAL	DIFFERENCE
Emergency Fund			
Holiday			
Investments			
Education Fund			
Travel			
Other Savings			
TOTAL SAVINGS			

EXPENSES	BUDGET	ACTUAL	DIFFERENCE
Mortgage/Rent Payment			
Home/Rental Insurance			
Auto Payment			
Groceries			
Utilities			
Cell Phone			
Cable/Internet			
Personal hygiene Items			
Pets			
Entertainment/Recreation			
Clothing			
Dry Cleaning			
Health Insurance			
Life Insurance			
Home Appliance Warranty			
Donations			
Membership/Subscription			
Daycare			
Credit Card Payments (Exclude previous expenses recorded in a specific category)			
Emergency Fund			
Travel			
Vacation			
Student Loan			
Gifts			
Fun Money			

Creditors Tracker

The Creditor Tracker is a great tool to help you keep track of your credit card balances and maintain peak financial health. The Creditor Tracker is especially valuable if you feel overwhelmed while looking at your credit report. It's easy to break up all that information when using the Creditor Tracker because there is a designated slot for you to put who the creditor is, the balance on the account, how much the interest rate is, and your monthly payment. By putting all this information into the Creditor Tracker, you can quickly see this information. Even better, after a few months, you can see if there are any patterns with your credit.

The Creditor Tracker will allow you to identify if your credit balance is getting too high or if your monthly payments are getting increasingly more expensive. The Creditor Tracker also lets you quickly see which of your credit cards has the highest or lowest interest rate, which can help you identify which account to tackle first if you're planning on applying the Debt Snowball Plan. Be sure to include the Creditor Tracker in your monthly credit report review.

CREDITORS TRACKER

MONTH ELEVEN

1. Write down your goals.
2. Make sure that you are specific about your goals.
3. Select the date you would like to have these goals completed.
4. What is the "why" for these goals?
5. Make sure your goals are measurable.
6. Create a MAP for your goals. **(Massive Action Plan)**
7. Monitor and track your progress.

USE THE SPACE BELOW AND THE FOLLOWING PAGES TO ANSWER THE QUESTIONS

_____

_____

_____

_____

_____

_____

_____

_____

_____

_____

_____

_____

_____

_____

_____

_____

_____

_____

_____

_____

_____

_____

_____

THIS MONTH'S GOALS

MONTH ELEVEN

I am so grateful for the ability to manifest money when I want it.

MONTH: _____

20 _____

Personal Goals

_____
_____
_____
_____
_____
_____

Financial Goals

_____
_____
_____
_____
_____
_____
_____

INCOME	BUDGET	ACTUAL	DIFFERENCE
Salary			
Gifts recieved			
Refunds			
Transfer from Savings			
Other Income			
TOTAL INCOME			

SAVINGS	BUDGET	ACTUAL	DIFFERENCE
Emergency Fund			
Holiday			
Investments			
Education Fund			
Travel			
Other Savings			
TOTAL SAVINGS			

EXPENSES	BUDGET	ACTUAL	DIFFERENCE
Mortgage/Rent Payment			
Home/Rental Insurance			
Auto Payment			
Groceries			
Utilities			
Cell Phone			
Cable/Internet			
Personal hygiene Items			
Pets			
Entertainment/Recreation			
Clothing			
Dry Cleaning			
Health Insurance			
Life Insurance			
Home Appliance Warranty			
Donations			
Membership/Subscription			
Daycare			
Credit Card Payments (Exclude previous expenses recorded in a specific category)			
Emergency Fund			
Travel			
Vacation			
Student Loan			
Gifts			
Fun Money			

Creditors Tracker

The Creditor Tracker is a great tool to help you keep track of your credit card balances and maintain peak financial health. The Creditor Tracker is especially valuable if you feel overwhelmed while looking at your credit report. It's easy to break up all that information when using the Creditor Tracker because there is a designated slot for you to put who the creditor is, the balance on the account, how much the interest rate is, and your monthly payment. By putting all this information into the Creditor Tracker, you can quickly see this information. Even better, after a few months, you can see if there are any patterns with your credit.

The Creditor Tracker will allow you to identify if your credit balance is getting too high or if your monthly payments are getting increasingly more expensive. The Creditor Tracker also lets you quickly see which of your credit cards has the highest or lowest interest rate, which can help you identify which account to tackle first if you're planning on applying the Debt Snowball Plan. Be sure to include the Creditor Tracker in your monthly credit report review.

CREDITORS TRACKER

MONTH TWELVE

<comment>...</comment>

1. Write down your goals.
2. Make sure that you are specific about your goals.
3. Select the date you would like to have these goals completed.
4. What is the "why" for these goals?
5. Make sure your goals are measurable.
6. Create a MAP for your goals. **(Massive Action Plan)**
7. Monitor and track your progress.

USE THE SPACE BELOW AND THE FOLLOWING PAGES TO ANSWER THE QUESTIONS

THIS MONTH'S GOALS

Everything I need to build wealth is available to me right now.

MONTH: _____

20 _____

Personal Goals

_____
_____
_____
_____
_____
_____

Financial Goals

_____
_____
_____
_____
_____
_____
_____
_____

INCOME	BUDGET	ACTUAL	DIFFERENCE
Salary			
Gifts recieved			
Refunds			
Transfer from Savings			
Other Income			
TOTAL INCOME			

SAVINGS	BUDGET	ACTUAL	DIFFERENCE
Emergency Fund			
Holiday			
Investments			
Education Fund			
Travel			
Other Savings			
TOTAL SAVINGS			

EXPENSES	BUDGET	ACTUAL	DIFFERENCE
Mortgage/Rent Payment			
Home/Rental Insurance			
Auto Payment			
Groceries			
Utilities			
Cell Phone			
Cable/Internet			
Personal hygiene Items			
Pets			
Entertainment/Recreation			
Clothing			
Dry Cleaning			
Health Insurance			
Life Insurance			
Home Appliance Warranty			
Donations			
Membership/Subscription			
Daycare			
Credit Card Payments (Exclude previous expenses recorded in a specific category)			
Emergency Fund			
Travel			
Vacation			
Student Loan			
Gifts			
Fun Money			

MONTHLY BUDGET TRACKER

Creditors Tracker

The Creditor Tracker is a great tool to help you keep track of your credit card balances and maintain peak financial health. The Creditor Tracker is especially valuable if you feel overwhelmed while looking at your credit report. It's easy to break up all that information when using the Creditor Tracker because there is a designated slot for you to put who the creditor is, the balance on the account, how much the interest rate is, and your monthly payment. By putting all this information into the Creditor Tracker, you can quickly see this information. Even better, after a few months, you can see if there are any patterns with your credit.

The Creditor Tracker will allow you to identify if your credit balance is getting too high or if your monthly payments are getting increasingly more expensive. The Creditor Tracker also lets you quickly see which of your credit cards has the highest or lowest interest rate, which can help you identify which account to tackle first if you're planning on applying the Debt Snowball Plan. Be sure to include the Creditor Tracker in your monthly credit report review.

CREDITORS TRACKER

NOTES

QUARTERLY CREDIT
SCORE CHECK IN

MONTH 10 CREDIT SCORE:

What factors caused my credit
score to increase or decrease?

MONTH 11 CREDIT SCORE:

P: _____

C: _____

L: _____

M: _____

R: _____

MONTH 12 CREDIT SCORE:

LEGEND:
P: Payment History
C: Credit Usage
L: Length of Credit
M: Mix of Credit
R: Recent Credit

- "Your Credit Score is the most important number in your life" —Dionne Perry

- "Too many people spend money they haven't earned, to buy things they don't want, to impress people that they don't like." —Will Rogers

- "You can't invest in your looks as your only thing because it's a depreciating asset. It's like putting money into a stock that's going down. Invest in your brain, invest in your talents. Those things can appreciate and they get better as you get older." —Rashida Jones

- "Don't be afraid to go outside the box. Don't be afraid to think outside the box. Don't be afraid to fail big, to dream big, but remember, dreams without goals are just dreams. And they ultimately fuel disappointment." —Denzel Washington

- "The most difficult thing is the decision to act, the rest is merely tenacity." —Amelia Earhart

- "Beware of little expenses; a small leak will sink a great ship." —Benjamin Franklin

- "You cannot escape the responsibility of tomorrow by evading it today." —Abraham Lincoln

- "To contract new debts is not the way to pay old ones." —George Washington

- "Your Credit Score Impacts Everything!" —Dionne Perry

- "The habit of saving is itself an education; it fosters every virtue, teaches self-denial, cultivates the sense of order, trains to forethought, and so broadens the mind." —T.T. Munger

- "Take one day at a time! Remember to Always make yourself a Priority! Stay Focused on what's important!" If you don't stay focused, it will show up later in life." —Ann James

_____

_____

_____

_____

_____

_____

_____

_____

_____

_____

_____

_____

_____

_____

YOUR TAKEAWAYS

PART FOUR

Glossary of Terms

Resources

GLOSSARY

Annual Percentage Rate (APR): The annual percentage rate you pay back for the entire year.

Bank: A financial institution that loans consumers money via a repayment plan.

Card issuer: A financial institution, bank, credit union or company that issues a line of credit to a consumer using a plastic card.

Cardholder: An individual to whom a business issued a card or who is authorized to use an issued card.

Collection: An effort by a collections department or agency to get a past-due debt repaid. Creditors usually report collection debts to credit agencies. Collection debts can impact your ability to borrow at reasonable rates.

Creditor: A person, organization or company that lends you money.

Consumer Financial Protection Bureau (CFPB): A federal agency charged with being a watchdog for consumer financial products, such as credit cards, payday loans, mortgages, and student loans.

Credit History: The record of use of debt. The three major credit agencies track individuals' credit histories and compile them into credit reports. Lenders (banks, credit unions, etc.) use credit histories to decide whether to provide customers with credit, and on what terms.

Credit Inquiry: Created when a lender accesses your credit record.

Credit Limit: The maximum amount of money the lender is willing to loan consumer.

Credit Report: An individual compilation of your credit history. The credit report details your history of borrowing, payment behavior and credit inquiries. Credit reports are viewed by lenders when deciding whether to extend credit to you and on what terms.

Credit Freeze: A service available to consumers through the credit agencies whereby consumers can "freeze" their credit, which prevents new accounts from being opened or someone accessing your credit report without your consent. Credit freeze is a useful tool if someone has stolen your identity.

Credit Score: A three-digit number that summarizes how well you repay debt to lenders. The higher the credit score number, the better. Individuals with high credit scores can qualify for larger loans with lower interest rates. Individuals with low credit scores may be turned down for credit or only be approved for a smaller amount with high interest rates.

Credit Reporting Agency (CRA): A company that tracks and sells your credit history to lenders.

Credit Utilization Ratio: Used in the calculation of your credit scores. It compares the amount of credit you are using to the total credit available to you.

Credit Union: A member-owned financial institution controlled by its members and operated on the principle of people helping people, usually providing its members financial services (i.e., loans, credit) at very competitive rates.

Credit Monitoring Service: A service that monitors your payment history and notifies you of suspicious or unusual activity on your credit report. Credit monitoring services charge a fee to monitor your credit.

Hard Inquiry: A hard inquiry occurs when you've applied for credit and the lender or creditor reviews your credit score to determine your credit worthiness.

Identity Theft: The deliberate use of someone else's identity, usually as a method to gain a financial advantage or obtain credit and other benefits in the other person's name.

Installment Credit: A type of agreement or contract that involves a loan to be repaid over a certain amount of time with a set number of scheduled payments. For example, a car loan is considered installment credit.

Interest Rate: The rate a bank or lender charges you to borrow its money. The higher your credit score the lower your interest rate. The lower your credit score the higher your interest rate. If your credit score is low, the bank or lender will charge you more money to borrow their money.

Late Payment Fee: A fee charged to a borrower who misses a minimum payment by the payment due date. In order to avoid late fees, always pay at least the minimum amount by the due date. Late payments will affect your credit score.

Lender: A person, organization or company that lends you money.

Line of Credit: The amount of money a financial institution, such as a bank or company, has agreed to lend you.

Open Credit: A pre-approved loan between a lender and a borrower. Open credit usually allows a borrower to make repeated withdrawals up to a certain limit.

Revolving Credit: A type of credit that does not have a fixed number of payments, in contrast to installment credit. For example, credit cards are considered revolving credit.

Social Security Number: A nine-digit number assigned to you for income reporting and other purposes. When applying for credit you have to list your social security number.

Soft Inquiry: A soft inquiry occurs when you check your credit score, or a lender checks your credit score for a preapproval offer. Soft inquires do not impact your credit scores.

RESOURCES

Follow Credit-Lit on these social media platforms for daily posts, freebies, new releases, and much more.

Website: www.Credit-Lit.com

Facebook: https://www.facebook.com/Credit-Lit

Instagram: https://www.instagram.com/credit.lit/

Twitter: https://twitter.com/litcredit

Pinterest: https://www.pinterest.com/instillpublishingmarketing

Tumblr: https://www.tumblr.com/blog/credit-lit

www.ingramcontent.com/pod-product-compliance
Lightning Source LLC
Chambersburg PA
CBHW052342210326
41597CB00037B/6224